A Teen Cookbook

Delicious and Easy Teen Recipes to Cook for Yourself

By
BookSumo Press

Published by
http://www.booksumo.com

LEGAL NOTES

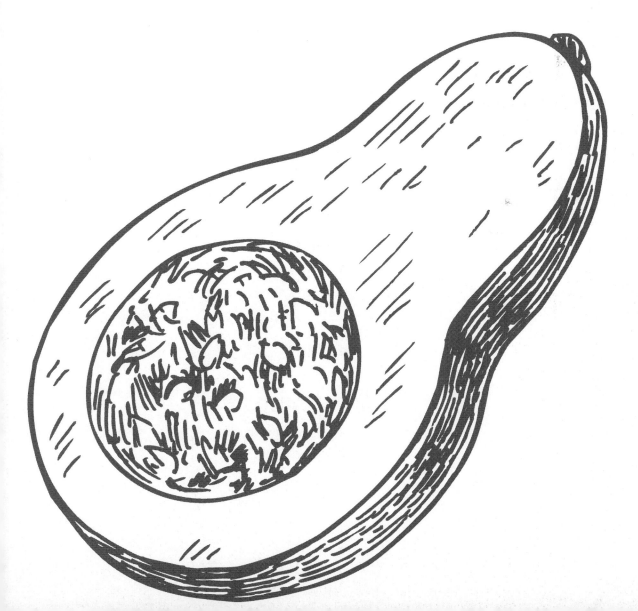

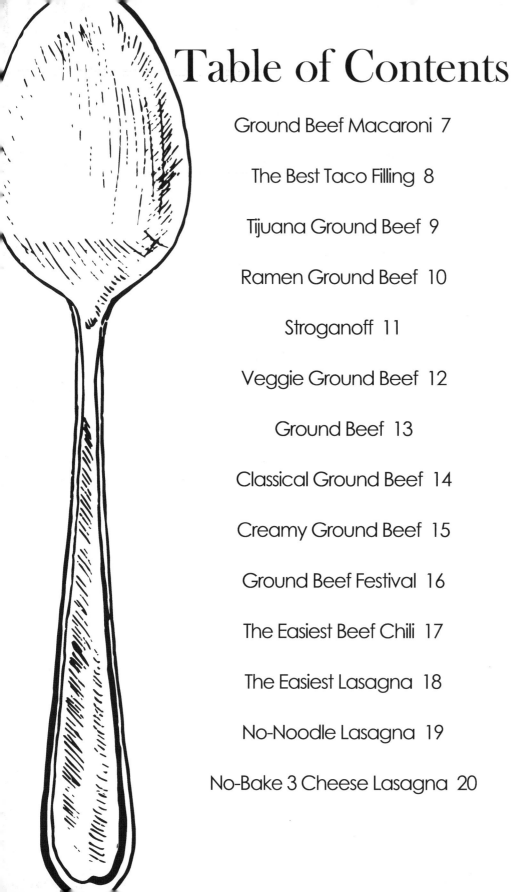

Table of Contents

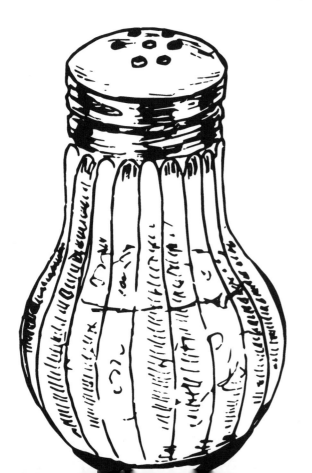
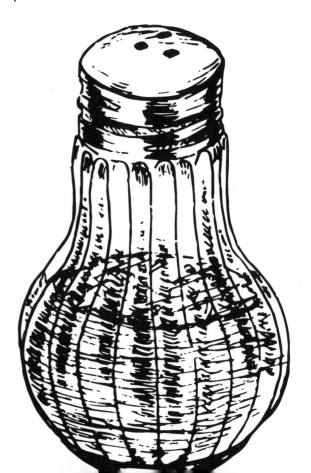

Ground Beef
Macaroni

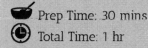

Prep Time: 30 mins
Total Time: 1 hr

Servings per Recipe: 6
Calories	570 kcal
Carbohydrates	72.9 g
Cholesterol	74 mg
Fat	15.5 g
Protein	35.2 g
Sodium	1492 mg

Ingredients

1 1/2 lbs lean ground beef
1 green bell pepper, diced
1 onion, diced

2 (29 ounce) cans tomato sauce
1 (16 ounce) package macaroni

Directions

1. Cook pasta according to the directions of package before draining it using a colander.
2. Cook ground beef over medium heat until brown before adding chopped onion and cooking it for another few minutes to get them soft.
3. Now add tomato sauce and green pepper before cooking it until pepper is soft.
4. Pour this sauce over pasta for serving.

THE BEST
Taco Filling

Prep Time: 5 mins
Total Time: 30 mins

Servings per Recipe: 4	
Calories	371 kcal
Carbohydrates	16.4 g
Cholesterol	85 mg
Fat	23.6 g
Protein	21 g
Sodium	1060 mg

Ingredients

1 lb lean ground beef
1 onion, diced
1/2 cup ketchup

1 package taco seasoning mix
2/3 cup cold water

Directions

1. Cook ground beef and onion over medium heat before stirring in ketchup, cold water and taco seasoning, and cooking all this for 20 minutes at low heat.
2. Serve.

Tijuana
Ground Beef (Mexican Style)

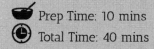

Prep Time: 10 mins
Total Time: 40 mins

Servings per Recipe: 4	
Calories	732 kcal
Carbohydrates	52.1 g
Cholesterol	171 mg
Fat	43.7 g
Protein	33.8 g
Sodium	592 mg

Ingredients

1 lb ground beef
1 cup salsa
1/2 cup water
1 green bell pepper, diced
1 bunch green onions, diced

1 (8 ounce) package wide egg noodles
1/2 cup sour cream
1/2 cup shredded Cheddar cheese
1 tomato, diced

Directions

1. Cook ground beef in a skillet until brown before stirring in water and salsa, and cooking all this for 10 minutes.
2. Now add onions and green pepper into the pan, and cook all this until you see that the veggies are tender before adding cooked noodles, grated cheese and sour cream.
3. Cover it up until the cheese melts before sprinkling some tomatoes.
4. Serve.

RAMEN
Ground Beef

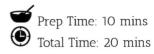 Prep Time: 10 mins
Total Time: 20 mins

Servings per Recipe: 4
Calories	368 kcal
Carbohydrates	30.2 g
Cholesterol	69 mg
Fat	17.1 g
Protein	23.3 g
Sodium	843 mg

Ingredients

1 lb ground beef
1 (3 ounce) package Oriental flavored ramen noodles

1 (14.5 ounce) can diced tomatoes
1 (10 ounce) can whole kernel corn

Directions

1. Cook beef over medium heat until you see that it is no longer pink before adding the flavor packet of the noodles, corn, noodles broken into pieces and tomatoes, and bring all this to boil.

2. Now turn down the heat to low and cook for 10 minutes or until the noodles are tender.

3. Serve.

Stroganoff

Prep Time: 15 mins
Total Time: 1 hr 15 mins

Servings per Recipe: 6	
Calories	524 kcal
Carbohydrates	11.3 g
Cholesterol	129 mg
Fat	40.5 g
Protein	27.6 g
Sodium	1923 mg

Ingredients

2 lbs ground beef
2 onions, diced
1 clove garlic, minced
1 (4.5 ounce) can mushrooms, drained
2 tsps salt
1/4 tsp ground black pepper
2 cups hot water

6 cubes beef bouillon
4 tbsps tomato paste
1 1/2 cups water
4 tbsps all-purpose flour

Directions

1. Cook ground beef, mushrooms, garlic and onions over medium heat until you see that onion is golden brown before adding salt and pepper.
2. Now add tomato paste, a mixture of flour and water, 2 cups of hot water and bouillon cubes before turning down the heat to low and cooking all this for one full hour.
3. Serve.

VEGGIE
Ground Beef

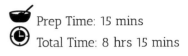

Prep Time: 15 mins
Total Time: 8 hrs 15 mins

Servings per Recipe: 6

Calories	354 kcal
Carbohydrates	45.9 g
Cholesterol	46 mg
Fat	10.4 g
Protein	22.4 g
Sodium	1465 mg

Ingredients

1 (32 fluid ounce) container beef broth, or more if needed
1 lb ground sirloin beef
1 (15.25 ounce) can whole kernel corn, drained
1 (15 ounce) can green beans, drained
1 (15 ounce) can peas, drained
1 (14 ounce) can tomato sauce
3 carrots, cut into bite-size pieces
2 potatoes, peeled and cut into bite-size pieces

1 onion, diced
1 large stalk celery, cut into bite-size pieces
1 clove garlic, minced
1 1/2 tbsps chopped fresh parsley
1/2 tsp celery seed
2 bay leaves
salt and ground black pepper to taste

Directions

1. In a slow cooker combine beef broth, garlic, ground sirloin, tomato sauce, corn, celery, celery seed, green beans, peas, carrots, potatoes, onion, parsley and bay leaves very thoroughly before cooking it for four full hours.
2. Now add broth and cook for another four hours before adding salt and pepper according to your taste.
3. Serve.

Ground Beef
(Slow Cooker)

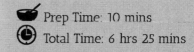

Prep Time: 10 mins

Total Time: 6 hrs 25 mins

Servings per Recipe: 20
Calories	188 kcal
Carbohydrates	14.5 g
Cholesterol	45 mg
Fat	8.5 g
Protein	13.9 g
Sodium	710 mg

Ingredients

3 lbs lean ground beef
1 large onion, diced
2 cloves garlic, minced
5 stalks celery, finely chopped
1 1/2 tsps salt
1/2 tsp ground black pepper

1 tbsp cider vinegar
2 tbsps prepared mustard
1/4 cup firmly packed brown sugar
3 1/2 cups ketchup

Directions

1. Cook ground beef over medium heat for about 15 minutes or until brown.
2. Now place this meat, onion, brown sugar, garlic, cider vinegar, celery, salt, black pepper, mustard and ketchup in a slow cooker and cook all this on low for 8 hours.
3. Serve.

CLASSICAL
Ground Beef

🥣 Prep Time: 10 mins
🕐 Total Time: 1 hr

Servings per Recipe: 4
Calories	252 kcal
Carbohydrates	4.5 g
Cholesterol	74 mg
Fat	15.9 g
Protein	21.6 g
Sodium	215 mg

Ingredients

1 lb lean ground beef
1 1/2 tbsps ketchup
1 tbsp prepared mustard
1 tbsp Worcestershire sauce
1 tbsp distilled white vinegar

1 small onion, grated
1/2 small green bell pepper, finely chopped

Directions

1. At first you need to set a grill to medium heat and put some oil before starting anything else.
2. Form patties from a mixture of ground beef, vinegar, ketchup, mustard, grated onion, Worcestershire sauce, and bell pepper very neatly.
3. Cook on the preheated grill for about 4 minutes each side.
4. Serve.

Creamy
Ground Beef

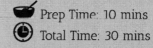 Prep Time: 10 mins

Total Time: 30 mins

Servings per Recipe: 8

Calories	201 kcal
Carbohydrates	8.5 g
Cholesterol	53 mg
Fat	10.8 g
Protein	16.3 g
Sodium	518 mg

Ingredients

1 lb ground beef
1/4 cup all-purpose flour
1 cube beef bouillon
3/4 tsp salt
1 pinch ground black pepper

2 1/4 cups milk
1/4 tsp Worcestershire sauce

Directions

1. Cook beef over medium heat for about 7 minutes or until brown before adding pepper, flour, salt and bouillon, and cook all this for five minutes.
2. Now add milk and Worcestershire sauce slowly into the pan before cooking all this for 10 minutes.
3. Serve.

GROUND BEEF
Festival

🥣 Prep Time: 10 mins
🕐 Total Time: 25 mins

Servings per Recipe: 4
Calories	815 kcal
Carbohydrates	50 g
Cholesterol	104 mg
Fat	56 g
Protein	29.9 g
Sodium	1795 mg

Ingredients

1 lb ground beef
1 tbsp garlic pepper seasoning
1 (15 ounce) can corn, drained
1 cup ranch dressing
1 cup salsa
1 tbsp dried oregano

shredded Cheddar cheese, or more to taste
2 cups cooked rice, or to taste(optional)

Directions

1. Cook beef and garlic over medium heat for about 7 minutes or until brown before adding corn, oregano, ranch dressing and salsa.
2. Cook all this for 10 minutes.
3. Pour this over rice for serving.

The Easiest
Beef Chili

Prep Time: 10 mins
Total Time: 2 hrs 10 mins

Servings per Recipe: 4
Calories	382 kcal
Carbohydrates	26.8 g
Cholesterol	70 mg
Fat	18.7 g
Protein	27 g
Sodium	1701 mg

Ingredients

1 lb ground beef
1 large onion, diced
1 (15 ounce) can ranch-style beans
1 (10 ounce) can diced tomatoes with green chili peppers

1 (1.25 ounce) package chili seasoning mix
salt and pepper to taste
2 tsps chili powder, or to taste
1 cup water, or as needed

Directions

1. Cook beef and onion until brown before adding beans, chili powder, diced tomatoes, pepper, chili seasoning, salt and water.
2. Turn down the heat to low and cook for two full hours.

THE EASIEST
Lasagna

Prep Time: 20 mins
Total Time: 1 hr 35 mins

Servings per Recipe: 12

Calories	293 kcal
Carbohydrates	26.1 g
Cholesterol	61 mg
Fat	12.5 g
Protein	17.8 g
Sodium	514 mg

Ingredients

1 lb ground beef
2 1/2 C. Shredded Mozzarella Cheese
1 container Ricotta Cheese
1/2 C. Parmesan Cheese
1/4 C. chopped fresh parsley
1 egg, beaten

1 jar spaghetti sauce
1 C. water
12 lasagna noodles, uncooked

Directions

1. Set your oven to 350 degrees before doing anything else.
2. Get a bowl, mix: beaten eggs, 1 1/4 C. mozzarella, parsley, 1 /4 C. parmesan, and ricotta.
3. Fry your beef until brown, remove excess oils. Combine in your tomato sauce, with 1 C. of water that has been shaken in the pasta sauce jar. Combine everything smoothly.
4. Get your baking dish and layer: 1 C. of meat mix, lasagna noodles, 1/3 ricotta, continue until all ingredients used.
5. Cook for 1 hr with a covering of foil. 20 mins without.
6. Enjoy.

No-Noodle
Lasagna

Prep Time: 20 mins
Total Time: 45 mins

Servings per Recipe: 8
Calories	461 kcal
Carbohydrates	35.3 g
Cholesterol	118 mg
Fat	20.3 g
Protein	32 g
Sodium	975 mg

Ingredients

1 lb ground beef
1 (26 oz) jar spaghetti sauce
1/2 tsp garlic powder
3 C. cooked rice, cooled
2 eggs, lightly beaten

3/4 C. shredded Parmesan cheese, divided
2 1/4 C. shredded mozzarella cheese
2 C. cottage cheese

Directions

1. Set your oven to 375 degrees before doing anything else.
2. Fry your beef until browned for 8 mins, and remove excess grease. Combine in your tomato sauce and also garlic powder.
3. Get a bowl, mix: 1/4 C. parmesan, whisked eggs, and rice.
4. Get a 2nd bowl, mix: 1/4 C. parmesan, cottage cheese, and 2 C. mozzarella
5. Layer the following in a dish: 1/2 rice, 1/2 cheese mix, 1/2 meat. Continue until dish is full. Then top with more mozzarella.
6. Cook for 25 mins, until sauce is simmering, and cheese melted.

NO-BAKE
3 Cheese Lasagna

Prep Time: 30 mins
Total Time: 2 hrs 30 mins

Servings per Recipe: 10	
Calories	521 kcal
Carbohydrates	50.3 g
Cholesterol	110 mg
Fat	20.6 g
Protein	33.1 g
Sodium	861 mg

Ingredients

1 (16 oz) package lasagna noodles
1 lb lean ground beef
1 1/2 (26 oz) jars spaghetti sauce
2 C. shredded mozzarella cheese
1/2 C. grated Parmesan cheese
1 (8 oz) container ricotta cheese

2 eggs
2 C. shredded mozzarella cheese

Directions

1. Boil lasagna in salted water for 7 min until al dente. Remove all water.
2. Fry your beef until brown, remove oil excess, mix in tomato sauce, simmer for 5 mins. Turn off heat.
3. Get a bowl, mix: beaten eggs, 2 C. mozzarella, ricotta, and parmesan.
4. Place half of your beef into the slow cooker first, then some lasagna noodles. Then 1/4 of the cheese mix, then 1/4 more sauce. Continue adding layers until nothing is lest. Topmost layer should be 2 C. of mozzarella.
5. Set slow cooker to high for 3 hours. Then set heat to low for 8 hours.
6. Enjoy.

Chocolaty Apples

🥣 Prep Time: 10 mins
🕐 Total Time: 40 mins

Servings per Recipe: 6
Calories   792 kcal
Fat   35.7 g
Carbohydrates   118.8g
Protein   14.9 g
Cholesterol   5 mg
Sodium   336 mg

Ingredients

6 Granny Smith apples
6 wooden sticks
1 (14 oz.) package individually wrapped caramels, unwrapped
2 tbsps water
1/2 tsp vanilla extract

3 C. trail mix
1 C. semisweet chocolate chips

Directions

1. Line a large cookie sheet with lightly greased aluminum foil.
2. Insert wooden sticks in each apple about 3/4 of the way into the stem end.
3. Arrange the apples onto the prepared cookie sheet.
4. In a pan, mix together water and caramel over low heat and cook, stirring occasionally, till the caramel is melted and smooth.
5. Stir in the vanilla and immediately, remove it from heat.
6. In a shallow dish, place the trail mix.
7. Dip each apple into the caramel mixture evenly and roll it in the trail mix evenly.
8. Place the apples into a cookie sheet and refrigerate to chill.
9. In a microwave safe bowl, microwave on high for about 30 seconds or melted completely, stirring occasionally.
10. Drizzle the apples with melted chocolate and chill again before serving.

CHOCOLATY
Cookies

Prep Time: 10 mins
Total Time: 1 hr

Servings per Recipe: 24	
Calories	171 kcal
Fat	10.7 g
Carbohydrates	19.2g
Protein	2.4 g
Cholesterol	29 mg
Sodium	62 mg

Ingredients

1 1/2 C. sifted whole wheat flour
1/2 tsp baking soda
1 1/3 C. packed brown sugar
2/3 C. unsalted butter
1/4 tsp salt
2 eggs
1 tsp vanilla extract

1 tbsp instant espresso powder
3 (1 oz.) squares unsweetened chocolate
3/4 C. halved macadamia nuts

Directions

1. Set your oven to 350 degrees F before doing anything else and lightly coat cookie sheets.
2. In a bowl, mix together flour, baking soda and salt.
3. In another bowl, add brown sugar and butter and beat till smooth.
4. Add the eggs, one at a time, beating continuously and stir in the vanilla and espresso.
5. Slowly, add the flour mixture into the egg mixture, beating continuously.
6. Meanwhile in a double broiler, melt the chocolate chips over low heat and let it cool.
7. Add melted chocolate and nuts into the flour mixture and stir till well combined.
8. Place the mixture onto prepared cookie sheets in a single layer.
9. Cook everything in the oven for about 12 minutes or till the top becomes golden brown.

Garden
Lasagna III (Broccoli, Carrots, & Corn)

🥣 Prep Time: 30 mins
🕐 Total Time: 1 hr 10 mins

Servings per Recipe: 10	
Calories	534 kcal
Carbohydrates	48.8 g
Cholesterol	103 mg
Fat	27 g
Protein	26.6 g
Sodium	1091 mg

Ingredients

1 box lasagna noodles
2 eggs, beaten
1 box part-skim ricotta cheese
2 cans condensed cream of mushroom soup
2 C. shredded Cheddar cheese
1 C. grated Parmesan cheese
1 C. sour cream
1 package herb and garlic soup mix

1 bag chopped frozen broccoli, thawed
1 bag frozen sliced carrots
1 bag frozen corn kernels

Directions

1. Set your oven to 375 degrees before anything else.
2. Boil noodles in water with salt for 10 mins. Remove all water, set aside.
3. Get a bowl, mix: soup mix, beaten eggs, sour cream, ricotta, parmesan, cheddar, and mushroom soup.
4. In your baking layer everything in the following manner: lasagna, cheese mix, carrots, corn, broccoli. Continue until all ingredients used. Cheese should be upmost layer.
5. Cook for 30, with a cover of foil. 10 mins without.
6. Enjoy.

PRETTY
Easy Lasagna

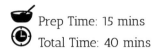

Prep Time: 15 mins
Total Time: 40 mins

Servings per Recipe: 8
Calories	386 kcal
Carbohydrates	29.6 g
Cholesterol	46 mg
Fat	19.3 g
Protein	22.1 g
Sodium	1135 mg

Ingredients

2 C. uncooked penne pasta
1 lb ground Italian sausage
1 (26 oz) jar spaghetti sauce
1 C. cottage cheese

2 C. shredded mozzarella cheese, divided

Directions

1. Set your oven to 350 degrees before doing anything else.
2. Boil your pasta for 8 mins in water and salt. While stir frying your Italian sausage for 10 mins. Then remove oil excesses.
3. Combine pasta, and tomato sauce, with your sausage. And simmer the mix for 3 mins.
4. Now coat a baking dish with nonstick spray. And layer 1/2 of the sauce and pasta at the bottom. Add a layer of cottage cheese, 1/2 mozzarella, add the rest of the pasta. Finally add the rest of the mozzarella.
5. Bake for 30 mins covered with foil. 5 mins without a covering.
6. Enjoy.

Microwave
Mexican Lasagna

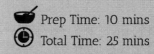 Prep Time: 10 mins

🕐 Total Time: 25 mins

Servings per Recipe: 10	
Calories	709 kcal
Carbohydrates	35.8 g
Cholesterol	143 mg
Fat	45.4 g
Protein	39.3 g
Sodium	1304 mg

Ingredients

11 oz lasagna noodles
1 lb lean ground beef
24 oz tomato sauce
1/2 C. water

1 (1 oz) package taco seasoning mix
8 C. shredded Cheddar cheese
1/2 C. minced tortilla chips

Directions

1. Boil your pasta for 10 mins in water and salt. Remove all water. Set aside.
2. Fry your beef until browned, and remove excess oils. Combine in some taco seasoning, then tomato and finally water. Lightly simmer for 6 mins.
3. Get your dish (must be able to fit in microwave), and layer in the following manner: lasagna noodles, beef mix, cheese. Continue until dish is full.
4. Microwave for 10 mins on the highest power setting covered with plastic wrap.
5. Garnish with tortilla chips.
6. Enjoy.

QUICK
Mozzarella Pasta Salad

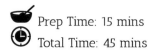

Prep Time: 15 mins
Total Time: 45 mins

Servings per Recipe: 4
Calories	451 kcal
Carbohydrates	47.6 g
Cholesterol	39 mg
Fat	21.8 g
Protein	17.3 g
Sodium	314 mg

Ingredients

1 (8 oz) package farfalle (bow tie) pasta
20 cherry tomatoes, halved
7 oz bocconcini (fresh mozzarella)
3/4 C. black olives

2 tbsps olive oil
6 fresh basil leaves
1 1/2 tsps fresh oregano leaves

Directions

1. Boil your bow tie pasta for 12 mins in salt and water. Then drain excess liquid. Let it set to room temp.
2. Get a bowl and mix: oregano, tomatoes, basil, olives, bocconcini, olive oil, and pasta.
3. Enjoy at room temp. or chilled.

Restaurant Style
Linguine

Prep Time: 10 mins
Total Time: 20 mins

Servings per Recipe: 4	
Calories	583 kcal
Carbohydrates	64.4 g
Cholesterol	205 mg
Fat	27.1 g
Protein	21 g
Sodium	373 mg

Ingredients

2 (8 oz) packages fresh linguine pasta
1 C. cream
4 oz smoked salmon, chopped
1 pinch freshly grated nutmeg (optional)
1 pinch ground black pepper, or to taste
(optional)

1 1/2 tbsps black caviar
1 bunch chopped flat leaf parsley

Directions

1. Boil your pasta in water and salt for 7 to 10 mins until al dente. Drain the liquid and set aside.
2. Get a saucepan and heat up your cream, then cook your salmon with pepper and nutmeg. Coat the pasta with this mixture. Add caviar as well.
3. Garnish everything with some parsley.
4. Enjoy.

EASY
Rigatoni

Prep Time: 15 mins
Total Time: 55 mins

Servings per Recipe: 8
Calories   295 kcal
Carbohydrates   48.8 g
Cholesterol   0 mg
Fat   8.3 g
Protein   8.9 g
Sodium   145 mg

Ingredients

1/4 C. olive oil
2 cloves garlic, diced
1 eggplant, peeled and cut into 1/2-inch cubes

1 (28 oz) can plum tomatoes with juice, chopped
1 (16 oz) package rigatoni pasta

Directions

1. Boil your rigatoni in salt and water for 12 mins until al dente. Remove excess liquid and set aside.
2. Get a frying pan: stir fry your garlic for 3 mins in olive oil. Add in your eggplants and fry for another 6 mins. Combine in your tomatoes and juice and simmer for 22 mins.
3. Cover pasta with eggplants and sauce.
4. Enjoy.

Quick
Stovetop Pasta

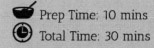

Prep Time: 10 mins
Total Time: 30 mins

Servings per Recipe: 4
Calories	328 kcal
Carbohydrates	47.4 g
Cholesterol	10 mg
Fat	10.2 g
Protein	11.7 g
Sodium	284 mg

Ingredients

1 (8 oz) package campanelle (little bells) pasta
1/2 C. ricotta cheese
2 tbsps olive oil

1/4 onion, chopped
1 (6.5 oz) can tomato sauce

Directions

1. Boil pasta in salt and water for 13 mins. Drain liquid and place in a bowl with ricotta, mix everything evenly.
2. Get a frying pan and fry onions in olive oil for 8 mins. Combine in your: tomato sauce. Stir fry for 4 mins.
3. Cover your noodles with the sauce, and let it sit for 7 mins.
4. Enjoy.

PECOS
Pasta

Prep Time: 10 mins
Total Time: 30 mins

Servings per Recipe: 4
Calories	315 kcal
Carbohydrates	49.2 g
Cholesterol	25 mg
Fat	9.7 g
Protein	11.9 g
Sodium	1336 mg

Ingredients

4 oz macaroni
1 tbsp butter
1 green bell pepper, chopped
1 onion, chopped
1 (8.75 oz) can whole kernel corn,
drained
1 (15 oz) can chili with beans

1 tsp salt
1 tsp ground black pepper

Directions

1. Boil your macaroni in salt and water for 10 mins. Remove liquid excesses.
2. Fry your, diced onions, and diced bell pepper in butter until onion is soft. Mix in some salt and pepper, chili beans, and corn. Lower your heating source and let everything simmer for 6 mins.
3. Finally combine in your macaroni and place a lid on the pan. Simmer for another 5 mins.
4. Enjoy.

A Light
Thai Inspired Pasta

Prep Time: 10 mins
Total Time: 15 mins

Servings per Recipe: 4
Calories	254 kcal
Carbohydrates	43.4 g
Cholesterol	0 mg
Fat	5.9 g
Protein	8.7 g
Sodium	43 mg

Ingredients

1 tbsp sesame oil
8 oz dry fettuccine pasta
1/2 tsp soy sauce
2 green onions, chopped
3/4 C. fresh bean sprouts
1 pinch cayenne pepper
1 pinch ground white pepper

1 pinch garlic powder
1 tbsp toasted sesame seeds

Directions

1. Boil your pasta for 10 mins in salt and water. Drain excess liquid. Set aside.
2. Get a frying pan, stir fry: pasta, soy sauce, garlic powder, green onions, pepper, bean sprouts, black pepper, and cayenne for 5 mins.
3. Garnish with toasted sesame.
4. Enjoy.

EASY
Mushroom Pasta

Prep Time: 3 mins
Total Time: 15 mins

Servings per Recipe: 5
Calories	526 kcal
Carbohydrates	64.2 g
Cholesterol	106 mg
Fat	22 g
Protein	18.2 g
Sodium	889 mg

Ingredients

1 (16 oz) package egg noodles
1 (10.75 oz) can condensed cream of
mushroom soup
1 C. cubed processed cheese
2 tbsps butter

1/4 C. milk
1 tsp garlic powder
salt and pepper to taste

Directions

1. Boil your pasta in salt and water for 10 mins. Remove excess liquid.
2. Get a pan and heat and stir until cheese melted: salt and pepper, mushroom soup, garlic powder, cheese, milk, and butter.
3. Once your cheese is melted mix in your noodles and heat for 1 more min. Coat evenly.
4. Enjoy.

Cheesy
Artichoke Pesto

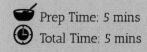 Prep Time: 5 mins
Total Time: 5 mins

Servings per Recipe: 12
Calories   118 kcal
Fat   11.9 g
Carbohydrates   1.1g
Protein   2 g
Cholesterol   3 mg
Sodium   92 mg

Ingredients

2 C. fresh basil leaves
2 tbsps crumbled feta cheese
1/4 C. freshly grated Parmesan cheese
1/4 C. pine nuts, toasted
1 artichoke heart, roughly chopped
2 tbsps chopped oil-packed sun-dried tomatoes

1/2 C. extra-virgin olive oil
1 pinch salt and black pepper to taste

Directions

1. In a large food processor, add all the ingredients except the oil and seasoning and pulse till combined.
2. While the motor is running slowly, add the oil and pulse till smooth.
3. Season with salt and black pepper and serve.

AMERICAN
Pesto

Prep Time: 15 mins
Total Time: 15 mins

Servings per Recipe: 6
Calories	389 kcal
Fat	35.8 g
Carbohydrates	5.4g
Protein	14.1 g
Cholesterol	14 mg
Sodium	343 mg

Ingredients

4 C. packed fresh basil leaves
1/4 C. Italian parsley
2 cloves garlic, peeled and lightly
crushed
1 C. pine nuts
1 1/2 C. shredded Parmigiano-Reggiano
cheese

1 tbsp fresh lemon juice
1/2 C. extra-virgin olive oil, or more as
needed
salt and ground black pepper to taste

Directions

1. In a food processor, add the parsley, basil, and garlic and pulse till chopped finely.
2. Add the pine nuts and pulse till copped very finely as well.
3. Add the cheese and pulse till combined.
4. While the motor is running, slowly mix in the lemon juice.
5. Then add the oil and pulse till well combined and smooth.
6. Season with salt and black pepper and serve.

Pasta
Pesto

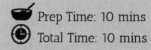 Prep Time: 10 mins
Total Time: 10 mins

Servings per Recipe: 16
Calories	113 kcal
Fat	11.1 g
Carbohydrates	1.2g
Protein	2.5 g
Cholesterol	4 mg
Sodium	82 mg

Ingredients

4 C. fresh baby spinach
1/2 C. pecans
2 cloves garlic
1 C. Parmesan cheese
1 tbsp lemon juice

1/2 C. extra virgin olive oil
1 pinch salt and freshly ground black pepper
to taste

Directions

1. In a large food processor, add all the ingredients except the oil and pulse till combined.
2. While the motor is running slowly, add the oil and pulse till well combined and smooth.

ASIAN
Peanut Pesto

Prep Time: 10 mins
Total Time: 10 mins

Servings per Recipe: 10
Calories   84 kcal
Fat   7.4 g
Carbohydrates   3.4g
Protein   1.9 g
Cholesterol   0 mg
Sodium   197 mg

Ingredients

1 bunch cilantro
1/4 C. peanut butter
3 cloves garlic, diced
3 tbsps extra-virgin olive oil
2 tbsps diced fresh ginger

1 1/2 tbsps fish sauce
1 tbsp brown sugar
1/2 tsp cayenne pepper

Directions

1. In a blender or food processor, add all the ingredients and pulse till smooth.

Pesto Spirals

Prep Time: 10 mins

Total Time: 20 mins

Servings per Recipe: 2

Calories	319 kcal
Fat	21.3 g
Carbohydrates	23.1g
Protein	12.1 g
Cholesterol	16 mg
Sodium	511 mg

Ingredients

1 tbsp olive oil
4 small zucchini, cut into noodle-shape strands
1/2 C. drained and rinsed canned garbanzo beans (chickpeas)

3 tbsps pesto, or to taste
salt and ground black pepper to taste
2 tbsps shredded white Cheddar cheese, or to taste

Directions

1. In a skillet, heat oil on medium heat.
2. Stir in the zucchini and cook for about 5-10 minutes or till all the liquid is absorbed.
3. Stir in the pesto and chickpeas and immediately reduce the heat to medium-low and cook for about 5 minutes or till the chickpeas and zucchini noodles are coated completely.
4. Stir in the salt and black pepper and immediately place the zucchini mixture onto serving plates.
5. Garnish the dish with the cheese and serve immediately.

SPICY
Pesto

Prep Time: 10 mins
Total Time: 10 mins

Servings per Recipe: 14
Calories	126 kcal
Fat	13 g
Carbohydrates	0.8g
Protein	2.2 g
Cholesterol	4 mg
Sodium	66 mg

Ingredients

1/4 C. walnuts
2 cloves garlic
2 C. packed fresh basil leaves
3/4 C. shredded Parmagiano-Reggiano cheese

1 jalapeno pepper, stem removed
2/3 C. olive oil
salt and ground black pepper to taste

Directions

1. In a food processor, add the garlic and walnuts and pulse till chopped finely.
2. Add the jalapeno, basil and cheese and pulse till well combined.
3. While the motor is running slowly, add the oil and pulse till well combined and smooth.
4. Season with salt and black pepper and serve.

Mushroom Pesto

Prep Time: 15 mins
Total Time: 30 mins

Servings per Recipe: 6
Calories	302 kcal
Fat	26.9 g
Carbohydrates	8.4g
Protein	10.8 g
Cholesterol	16 mg
Sodium	474 mg

Ingredients

2 tbsps butter
1 lb mixed fresh mushrooms (such as cremini, button, oyster, and portobello), quartered
1 shallot, chopped
1 C. toasted pine nuts
1/4 C. extra-virgin olive oil
1/4 C. vegetable broth

3 cloves garlic, chopped
1 tbsp freshly squeezed lemon juice
1 tsp kosher salt
1/2 tsp freshly ground black pepper
1/2 C. Parmesan cheese, grated

Directions

1. In a pan, melt the butter on medium heat.
2. Stir in the shallots and mushrooms and cook for about 5-7 minutes or till the mushrooms become golden brown.
3. Remove from heat and keep aside to cool for about 10 minutes.
4. In a blender, add the cooked mushroom mixture and remaining ingredients except cheese and pulse till grounded finely.
5. Transfer the mixture into a bowl and stir in the cheese before serving.

CREAMY
Lettuce Pesto

Prep Time: 10 mins
Total Time: 10 mins

Servings per Recipe: 8

Calories	113 kcal
Fat	9.6 g
Carbohydrates	1.5g
Protein	5.9 g
Cholesterol	12 mg
Sodium	215 mg

Ingredients

1/2 clove garlic
1/3 C. walnuts
3 oz. watercress, rinsed and dried
1 C. freshly grated Parmesan cheese

2 tbsps mayonnaise

Directions

1. In a food processor, add all the ingredients and pulse till a smooth paste forms.

Popcorn
American Style

Prep Time: 30 mins
Total Time: 1 hr 30 mins

Servings per Recipe: 20	
Calories	253 kcal
Fat	14 g
Carbohydrates	32.8g
Protein	0.9 g
Cholesterol	24 mg
Sodium	340 mg

Ingredients

1 C. butter
2 C. brown sugar
1/2 C. corn syrup
1 tsp salt

1/2 tsp baking soda
1 tsp vanilla extract
5 quarts popped popcorn

Directions

1. Set your oven to 250 degrees F before doing anything else.
2. In a large heatproof bowl, place the popcorn.
3. In a pan, melt the butter on medium heat and stir in the corn syrup, brown sugar and salt.
4. Bring to a boil, stirring continuously and cook for about 4 minutes.
5. Remove everything from the heat and immediately, stir in the vanilla extract and baking powder.
6. Place the mixture over the popcorn and stir to combine.
7. Transfer the popcorn mixture into 2 large shallow baking dishes.
8. Cook everything in the oven for about 1 hour, stirring every 15 minutes.
9. Remove everything from the oven and keep it aside to cool completely.
10. Break the dish into the desired size pieces and serve.

KIDS
Favorite Chocolaty Popcorn

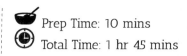 Prep Time: 10 mins

Total Time: 1 hr 45 mins

Servings per Recipe: 16
Calories	185 kcal
Fat	12 g
Carbohydrates	18.9g
Protein	3 g
Cholesterol	15 mg
Sodium	164 mg

Ingredients

2 quarts popped popcorn
1 C. peanuts
3/4 C. sugar
1/4 C. corn syrup

1/4 C. cocoa powder
1/2 C. butter
1 tsp vanilla

Directions

1. Set your oven to 250 degrees F before doing anything else and grease a 15x10-inch baking dish.
2. In a large heatproof bowl, place the popcorn and peanuts.
3. In a pan, mix together the butter, corn syrup, sugar and cocoa powder on medium-high heat.
4. Bring to a boil, stirring continuously and cook for about 2 minutes.
5. Remove everything from the heat and immediately, stir in the vanilla extract.
6. Place the mixture over the popcorn and stir to combine.
7. Transfer the popcorn mixture into prepared baking dish.
8. Cook everything in the oven for about 30 minutes, stirring occasionally.
9. Remove everything from the oven and keep it aside to cool completely.
10. Break the dish into the desired size pieces and serve.

Caesar
Parmesan Pasta Salad

Prep Time: 15 mins
Total Time: 30 mins

Servings per Recipe: 12	
Calories	291 kcal
Carbohydrates	32.6 g
Cholesterol	6 mg
Fat	14.6 g
Protein	8.5 g
Sodium	728 mg

Ingredients

1 (16 ounce) package rotini pasta
1 cup Italian-style salad dressing
1 cup creamy Caesar salad dressing
1 cup grated Parmesan cheese

1 red bell pepper, diced
1 green bell pepper, chopped
1 red onion, diced

Directions

1. Cook pasta in salty boiling water for about 10 minutes until tender before draining it.

2. Mix pasta, red bell pepper, Italian salad dressing, Caesar dressing, Parmesan cheese, green bell pepper and red onion very thoroughly before refrigerating for a few hours.

3. Serve.

EASY-TO-PREPARE
Popcorn

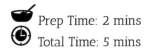 Prep Time: 2 mins

Total Time: 5 mins

Servings per Recipe: 3
Calories	137 kcal
Fat	3.1 g
Carbohydrates	24.6g
Protein	4.1 g
Cholesterol	0 mg
Sodium	389 mg

Ingredients

1/2 C. unpopped popcorn
1 tsp vegetable oil
1/2 tsp salt, or to taste

Directions

1. In a small bowl, add the popcorn, oil and salt and toss to coat.
2. In a brown paper lunch sack, place the popcorn and fold the top twice to seal the popcorn mixture.
3. Microwave on very high for about 2 1/2-3 minutes.

Healthy
Pasta Salad

🍲 Prep Time: 15 mins
🕐 Total Time: 30 mins

Servings per Recipe: 12	
Calories	289 kcal
Carbohydrates	34.6 g
Cholesterol	8 mg
Fat	13.9 g
Protein	10 g
Sodium	764 mg

Ingredients

1 (16 ounce) package uncooked rotini pasta
1 (16 ounce) bottle Italian salad dressing
2 cucumbers, chopped
6 tomatoes, chopped

1 bunch green onions, chopped
4 ounces grated Parmesan cheese
1 tbsp Italian seasoning

Directions

1. Cook pasta in salty boiling water for about 10 minutes until tender before draining it.
2. Coat a mixture of pasta, green onions, cucumbers and tomatoes with a mixture of parmesan cheese and Italian seasoning very thoroughly before refrigerating it covered for a few hours.
3. Serve.

VEGETABLE
Pasta Salad

Prep Time: 10 mins
Total Time: 25 mins

Servings per Recipe: 8

Calories	181 kcal
Carbohydrates	38.1 g
Cholesterol	0 mg
Fat	0.7 g
Protein	5.4 g
Sodium	238 mg

Ingredients

10 ounces fusilli pasta
1 onion, chopped
1 green bell pepper, chopped
2 tomatoes, chopped

1 cup chopped mushrooms
3/4 cup fat free Italian-style dressing

Directions

1. Cook pasta in salty boiling water for about 10 minutes until tender before draining it.

2. Mix pasta, mushrooms, onions, tomatoes and bell pepper very thoroughly before refrigerating for at least one hour.

3. Serve.

Italian Chicken Pasta Salad

🥣 Prep Time: 10 mins
🕐 Total Time: 2 hrs 35 mins

Servings per Recipe: 6	
Calories	218 kcal
Carbohydrates	20.4 g
Cholesterol	18 mg
Fat	11.4 g
Protein	9.6 g
Sodium	654 mg

Ingredients

1 cup seashell pasta
1 cup chopped, cooked chicken meat
3 green onions, chopped into 1 inch pieces
1 red bell pepper, chopped
1 cup sliced black olives

1 cucumber, peeled and chopped
2/3 cup Italian-style salad dressing
1/4 cup sunflower seeds(optional)

Directions

1. Cook pasta in salty boiling water for about 10 minutes until tender before draining it.
2. Coat mixture of pasta, bell pepper, chicken, green onions, olives and cucumber with dressing very thoroughly before refrigerating for at least 2 hours.
3. Serve.

ROTINI
Cucumber Pasta Salad

 Prep Time: 15 mins

Total Time: 2 hrs 30 mins

Servings per Recipe: 8

Calories	297 kcal
Carbohydrates	43.9 g
Cholesterol	0 mg
Fat	10.6 g
Protein	7.2 g
Sodium	608 mg

Ingredients

14 ounces uncooked rotini pasta
2 cucumbers, chopped
1/2 onion, finely chopped
10 cherry tomatoes, quartered

3/4 cup pitted black olives, sliced
1 cup Italian-style salad dressing

Directions

1. Cook rotini in salty boiling water for about 10 minutes until tender before draining it.
2. Coat a mixture of pasta, olives, cucumbers, tomatoes and onion with Italian dressing very thoroughly before refrigerating for at least two hours.
3. Serve.

The Simple
Frittata Formula

Prep Time: 5 mins
Total Time: 25 mins

Servings per Recipe: 1
Calories	239.0 kcal
Cholesterol	440.7mg
Sodium	408.4mg
Carbohydrates	3.0g
Protein	18.0g

Ingredients

2 large eggs
salt
fresh ground pepper
2 tbsps shredded cheese

2/3 C. vegetables
2 tbsps fresh herbs

Directions

1. Set your oven to 350 degrees before doing anything else.
2. Get a bowl, combine: herbs, cheese, and eggs.
3. Coat a skillet with nonstick spray then add in your veggies.
4. Cook the veggies for 1 min then add in the egg mix.
5. Set the heat to low and let the bottom of the eggs set with a lid on the pan for 10 mins.
6. Now place the frittata in the oven for 5 to 10 more mins until the top is set.
7. Enjoy.

EASY
Bacon Frittata

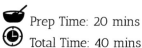 Prep Time: 20 mins
Total Time: 40 mins

Servings per Recipe: 4
Calories   297.4 kcal
Cholesterol   401.7mg
Sodium   317.8mg
Carbohydrates   5.5g
Protein   16.0g

Ingredients

1 red pepper, chopped
6 green onions, chopped
8 slices turkey bacon, sliced into small
pieces
8 eggs
1/2 C. half-and-half

1 tbsp butter
salt and pepper

Directions

1. Set your oven to 350 degrees before doing anything else.
2. Now begin to fry your bacon in butter until it is fully done. Then add in the veggies and let them cook until they are soft.
3. At the same time get a bowl, whisk: pepper, salt, half and half, and the eggs.
4. Beat the mix until it is smooth then pour it into the pan once the veggies are soft.
5. Let the frittata cook for about 6 mins until the bottom is set then place everything into the oven for 12 mins.
6. Enjoy.

The Simple
Chives Frittata

🥣 Prep Time: 10 mins
🕐 Total Time: 40 mins

Servings per Recipe: 8	
Calories	128.9 kcal
Cholesterol	224.0mg
Sodium	146.0mg
Carbohydrates	1.1g
Protein	9.8g

Ingredients

8 eggs
2 tbsps water
1 C. shredded colby-monterey jack cheese, divided

1/2 C. fresh chives, chopped
1/2 C. minced red bell pepper
1/2 tsp fresh ground black pepper

Directions

1. Set your oven to 350 degrees before doing anything else.
2. Get a bowl and beat your eggs in it then add in: 1/2 C. of cheese, herbs, black pepper, and bell pepper.
3. Combine the mix until it is smooth then coat a pie dish with nonstick spray.
4. Add the wet mix to the pan and evenly then top it with the rest of the cheese.
5. Cook the frittata in the oven for 35 mins then top it with some more herbs.
6. Enjoy.

THE PEPPER JACK
Pepper Frittata

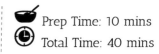

Prep Time: 10 mins
Total Time: 40 mins

Servings per Recipe: 8
Calories   128.9 kcal
Cholesterol   224.0mg
Sodium   146.0mg
Carbohydrates   1.1g
Protein   9.8g

Ingredients

8 eggs
2 tbsps water
1 C. shredded pepper jack cheese,
divided
1/2 C. fresh tarragon

1/2 C. minced red bell pepper
1/2 tsp fresh ground black pepper

Directions

1. Set your oven to 350 degrees before doing anything else.
2. Get a bowl, combine: water and eggs.
3. Stir the mix until it is smooth then add in half a C. of cheese, tarragon, black pepper, and bell peppers.
4. Stir the mix until it is smooth then top it with the rest of the cheese.
5. Enter everything into a pie dish then cook the frittata in the oven for 35 mins.
6. Enjoy.

The Garden
Frittata

Prep Time: 5 mins

Total Time: 15 mins

Servings per Recipe: 4

Calories	211.5 kcal
Cholesterol	339.7mg
Sodium	370.3mg
Carbohydrates	4.7g
Protein	14.4g

Ingredients

4 small yellow squash
1 tbsp butter
6 eggs
1/2 C. cheddar cheese, shredded

1 tsp italian seasoning
1/4 tsp salt
1/2 tsp pepper

Directions

1. Cut your squash into thin slices. Then fry them in butter until crispy.
2. Get a bowl, combine: pepper, eggs, salt, Italian seasoning, and shredded cheese.
3. Add the egg mix to the squash in the pan and let the mix cook for 10 mins with a low level of heat and a lid on the pot.
4. Now place the frittata under the broiler for 3 mins to cook the top.
5. Enjoy.

ITALIAN
Pasta Frittata

Prep Time: 2 mins
Total Time: 17 mins

Servings per Recipe: 2
Calories	891.3 kca
Cholesterol	539.3mg
Sodium	822.7mg
Carbohydrates	65.7g
Protein	34.9g

Ingredients

6 oz. cooked pasta, coated with tomato sauce
4 eggs
2 oz. shredded parmesan cheese
3 oz. butter

salt & freshly ground black pepper

Directions

1. Get a bowl combine: cheese, eggs, and pasta.
2. Stir the mix then add in some pepper and salt.
3. Melt 1/2 of your butter in a frying pan then add the pasta mix, set the heat to low, and let everything cook for 12 mins.
4. Invert the pan over a plate then place the opposite side of the frittata facing downwards in the pan.
5. Continue frying everything for 4 more mins.
6. Enjoy.

Tuna Breakfast

🥣 Prep Time: 10 mins

🕐 Total Time: 15 mins

Servings per Recipe: 1	
Calories	833 kcal
Fat	47.1 g
Carbohydrates	33.2g
Protein	66.3 g
Cholesterol	133 mg
Sodium	1098 mg

Ingredients

1 (6 oz.) can chunk light tuna, drained
2 tbsp mayonnaise
1 tsp Dijon mustard
1 bagel, split and toasted

1/2 C. shredded Cheddar cheese

Directions

1. Set your oven to 300 degrees F before doing anything else.
2. In a bowl, add the tuna, mayonnaise and mustard and with a fork, mash till well combined.
3. Spread tuna mixture over each bagel half evenly and sprinkle with the shredded Cheddar cheese.
4. Arrange the bagel halves onto a baking sheet.
5. Cook in the oven for about 5 minutes.

JALAPENO
Bites

Prep Time: 15 mins
Total Time: 30 mins

Servings per Recipe: 8
Calories	73 kcal
Fat	6.9 g
Carbohydrates	1.7g
Protein	2 g
Cholesterol	14 mg
Sodium	158 mg

Ingredients

18 fresh jalapeno peppers, halved
lengthwise and seeded
1 (5.25 oz.) package frozen vegetarian
bacon strips, thawed
toothpicks

1 (8 oz.) package cream cheese, softened

Directions

1. Set your oven to 350 degrees F before doing anything else and lightly coat a baking sheet.
2. Divide the cream cheese into each jalapeno half evenly and wrap with 1 bacon strip and secure with a toothpick.
3. Place the jalapeno halves onto the prepared baking sheet in a single layer and cook everything in the oven for about 12 minutes or till crisp.

Baked
Seattle Snack

🥣 Prep Time: 10 mins
🕐 Total Time: 25 mins

Servings per Recipe: 18
Calories   198.4
Cholesterol   13.5mg
Sodium   152.5mg
Carbohydrates   21.4g
Protein   4.0g

Ingredients

18 C. popped popcorn, use light butter microwave popcorn
1 C. salted peanuts, could also use honey roasted instead

1/2 C. butter
3/4 C. brown sugar
1/4 C. molasses

Directions

1. Set your oven to 350 degrees F before doing anything else and line 2 large baking sheets with wax paper.
2. Divide the popped popcorn between both prepared baking sheets and top each with peanuts evenly.
3. Melt butter in a small pan on medium heat then stir in the molasses and brown sugar.
4. Bring everything to a gentle simmer and cook for 5 minutes.
5. Remove the mix from the heat and place over the popcorn evenly.
6. Cook everything in the oven for about 15 minutes, stirring every 3 minutes.

THE SPRING TIME
Sandwich

Prep Time: 25 mins
Total Time: 25 mins

Servings per Recipe: 4
Calories	811 kcal
Fat	56.1 g
Carbohydrates	29.6g
Protein	46.3 g
Cholesterol	204 mg
Sodium	908 mg

Ingredients

1/2 C. mayonnaise
1/4 C. blue cheese dressing
8 slices multigrain bread
2 cooked chicken breasts, sliced
1 ripe avocado, sliced

8 slices cooked turkey bacon
2 hard-boiled eggs, minced
4 lettuce leaves

Directions

1. Get a bowl and mix the blue cheese with some mayo.
2. Coat your bread with 2 tbsps of this mix.
3. Place a quarter of your chicken breast on four pieces of bread.
4. Then layer the following on each piece: lettuce, avocado, hard-boiled egg, bacon, another piece of bread.
5. Enjoy with some blue cheese on the side for dipping.

Summer
Sandwich

Prep Time: 15 mins
Total Time: 20 mins

Servings per Recipe: 8
Calories	386 kcal
Fat	21.5 g
Carbohydrates	31.6 g
Protein	16.8 g
Cholesterol	40 mg
Sodium	738 mg

Ingredients

1 (1 lb) loaf ciabatta bread
3/4 C. pesto
8 oz. fontina cheese, sliced
2 ripe tomatoes, sliced

4 leaves butter lettuce

Directions

1. Turn on your oven's broiler to low if possible.
2. Cut your bread in half. Coat one side with some pesto then layer the following on the other side: tomato, and fontina cheese.
3. Place the pieces of bread which have cheese under the broiler until the cheese has melted.
4. Top this piece with some lettuce.
5. Form sandwiches then cut them in half for serving.
6. Enjoy.

THE FLUFFY
Sandwich

Prep Time: 4 mins
Total Time: 5 mins

Servings per Recipe: 1
Calories	373 kcal
Fat	18.1 g
Carbohydrates	43.5g
Protein	12.1 g
Cholesterol	0 mg
Sodium	502 mg

Ingredients

2 tbsps peanut butter
2 slices bread
2 1/2 tbsps marshmallow cream

Directions

1. Lay two pieces of bread flat on a working surface.
2. Coat one piece of bread with peanut butter, and another piece with marshmallow cream.
3. Now microwave the pieces of bread for 30 secs with the highest power setting.
4. Form the pieces into a sandwich and enjoy with milk.

Easy Egg and American Sandwich

Prep Time: 1 min
Total Time: 5 mins

Servings per Recipe: 1	
Calories	318 kcal
Fat	15.8 g
Carbohydrates	26.9 g
Protein	16.9 g
Cholesterol	214 mg
Sodium	839 mg

Ingredients

1 egg
1 tbsp milk
2 slices white bread
salt and pepper to taste (optional)

1 slice American cheese

Directions

1. Get a bowl, and mix: whisked eggs, salt, pepper, and milk.
2. Microwave the mix for 90 secs in the microwave with the highest power setting.
3. Simultaneously toast your bread slices then add your egg to the toasted bread.
4. Before forming a sandwich top the egg with a piece of cheese.
5. Now heat everything in the microwave for 30 more secs.
6. Enjoy.

THE MOSCOW
Sandwich

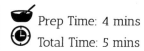

Prep Time: 4 mins
Total Time: 5 mins

Servings per Recipe: 1

Calories	535 kcal
Fat	28.8 g
Carbohydrates	38.7g
Protein	30.8 g
Cholesterol	88 mg
Sodium	2472 mg

Ingredients

2 slices American cheese
2 slices white bread, toasted
3 slices deli-style sliced turkey breast

2 tbsps Russian salad dressing

Directions

1. On one piece of toasted bread put 1 piece of cheese.
2. Now heat it in the microwave for 30 secs.
3. Layer some turkey on the cheese and on the remaining piece of bread coat it with some Russian dressing.
4. Form a sandwich and enjoy.

Fruity Neufchatel Sandwich

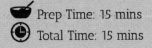

Prep Time: 15 mins
Total Time: 15 mins

Servings per Recipe: 8
Calories	289 kcal
Fat	10.3 g
Carbohydrates	40.4g
Protein	10.6 g
Cholesterol	21 mg
Sodium	344 mg

Ingredients

1 (8 oz.) package Neufchatel cheese, softened
1/4 C. crushed pineapple, drained
4 bananas, sliced

1/2 C. shredded coconut
16 slices whole-grain bread

Directions

1. Get a bowl, mix: pineapple and cheese.
2. Coat one piece of bread with this mix and then layer some banana on top of it, top everything with a final layer of coconut.
3. Form a sandwich with another piece of bread.
4. Enjoy.

THE LITTLE
Tike Sandwich

Prep Time: 10 mins
Total Time: 10 mins

Servings per Recipe: 3
Calories	250 kcal
Fat	15.8 g
Carbohydrates	21.4g
Protein	8.5 g
Cholesterol	0 mg
Sodium	104 mg

Ingredients

1/4 C. peanut butter, or to taste
1 Gala apple, cored and sliced
horizontally into discs

1/2 C. granola

Directions

1. Apply a coating of peanut butter to each piece of apple. Then top everything with some granola.
2. Lay two pieces of apples together, joining them at the granola and peanut butter.
3. Repeat with the remaining apple pieces to form apple sandwiches.
4. Enjoy.

The Americana
Sandwich

🍳 Prep Time: 5 mins
🕐 Total Time: 10 mins

Servings per Recipe: 1
Calories	488 kcal
Fat	32.1 g
Carbohydrates	29.2g
Protein	21.3 g
Cholesterol	91 mg
Sodium	1081 mg

Ingredients

2 slices sourdough bread
1 tbsp butter
1 tbsp grated Parmesan cheese
1 slice American cheese

1 slice Cheddar cheese

Directions

1. Coat a single side of each piece of bread with some butter. Then add some parmesan to this side and place it downwards in a frying pan.
2. Now place a piece of American and cheddar cheese on top of the bread.
3. Add another piece of bread on top of the cheese with its buttered side facing upwards to form a sandwich.
4. Fry the sandwich for a few mins until it is golden on both sides.
5. Enjoy.

CORNED BEEF
and Sauerkraut Sandwich

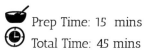

Prep Time: 15 mins
Total Time: 45 mins

Servings per Recipe: 4
Calories	657 kcal
Fat	40.3 g
Carbohydrates	43.5g
Protein	32.1 g
Cholesterol	115 mg
Sodium	1930 mg

Ingredients

2 tbsps butter
8 slices rye bread
8 slices deli sliced corned beef
8 slices Swiss cheese

1 C. sauerkraut, drained
1/2 C. Thousand Island dressing

Directions

1. Coat one side of your bread with butter. Then coat the opposite side with dressing.
2. Place the following on four pieces of bread: 1 piece of Swiss, one fourth C. sauerkraut, 2 pieces of corned beef, the rest of the Swiss.
3. Add another piece of bread and make sure the buttered sides are facing outwards.
4. Fry the sandwiches for 15 mins on each side.
5. Enjoy.

Roast Beef
and Provolone
Sandwich

🥄 Prep Time: 5 mins
🕐 Total Time: 15 mins

Servings per Recipe: 4
Calories   548 kcal
Fat   22.6 g
Carbohydrates   40.5g
Protein   44.6 g
Cholesterol   94 mg
Sodium   2310 mg

Ingredients

1 (10.5 oz.) can beef consommé
1 C. water
1 lb thinly sliced deli roast beef
8 slices provolone cheese

4 hoagie rolls, split lengthwise

Directions

1. Set your oven to 350 degrees before doing anything else.
2. Open your rolls and place them in a casserole dish.
3. Now combine water and beef consommé in a pan to make a broth.
4. Cook your beef in this mixture for 5 mins.
5. Then divide the meat between your rolls and top them with cheese.
6. Cook the rolls in the oven for 6 mins.
7. Enjoy the sandwiches dipped in broth.

OREGANO
Mozzarella Sandwich

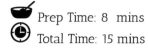 Prep Time: 8 mins

Total Time: 15 mins

Servings per Recipe: 6

Calories	394 kcal
Fat	18.3 g
Carbohydrates	42g
Protein	15 g
Cholesterol	46 mg
Sodium	1032 mg

Ingredients

1/4 C. unsalted butter
1/8 tsp garlic powder (optional)
12 slices white bread
1 tsp dried oregano

1 (8 oz.) package shredded mozzarella cheese
1 (24 oz.) jar vodka marinara sauce

Directions

1. Turn on the broiler before doing anything else.
2. Get a baking dish and lay half of your bread pieces in it.
3. On top of each piece of bread put some mozzarella. Then top the cheese with the remaining pieces of bread.
4. With a butter knife coat each sandwich with some butter. Then season the butter by applying some oregano and garlic powder.
5. Broil the sandwiches for 4 mins then flip it and apply more butter, oregano, and garlic to its opposite side.
6. Continue broiling the sandwich for another 4 mins.
7. Enjoy with the marinara as a dip.

A Class
President's Lunch

Prep Time: 10 mins
Total Time: 10 mins

Servings per Recipe: 1
Calories	211.2
Fat	5.9g
Cholesterol	212.0mg
Sodium	70.9mg2
Carbohydrates	34.1g
Protein	9.1g

Ingredients

lettuce leaf, washed and well dried
1 scoop low fat cottage cheese
4 rye crisps
1 hard-boiled egg, cut into wedges

1/4 fresh pineapple, diced
1/2 fresh peach, peeled and sliced
1/4 fresh papaya, peeled and sliced

Directions

1. Arrange the lettuce leaf onto a plate.
2. Place the cottage cheese in center and arrange the crackers around the edges.
3. Place the egg and fruits around the outside of the cottage cheese in a circle.
4. Serve immediately.

CHERRY
Chicken
Quesadillas

 Prep Time: 10 mins
Total Time: 26 mins

Servings per Recipe: 4
Calories	618 kcal
Fat	33 g
Carbohydrates	39 g
Protein	39.6 g
Cholesterol	112 mg
Sodium	860 mg

Ingredients

4 flour tortillas
2 C. shredded Cheddar cheese
2 C. cooked shredded chicken
1 C. fresh spinach

1/2 C. chopped cherry tomatoes
1 tbsp vegetable oil

Directions

1. Set your oven to 350 degrees F before doing anything else.
2. Arrange the tortillas on a baking sheet and spread 1/2 C. of the Cheddar cheese over each.
3. Cook in the oven for about 5 minutes.
4. Remove from the oven.
5. Heat a large skillet on medium heat and cook the chicken, spinach and tomatoes for about 5 minutes.
6. Place the chicken mixture over each tortilla evenly and fold in half.
7. Grease the same skillet with a thin layer of the oil and heat on medium heat.
8. Cook the tortillas in batches for about 3 minutes per side.

Morelia
Quesadillas

🥣 Prep Time: 10 mins
🕐 Total Time: 35 mins

Servings per Recipe: 4
Calories	450 kcal
Fat	26 g
Carbohydrates	40.9 g
Protein	13.9 g
Cholesterol	40 mg
Sodium	726 mg

Ingredients

1 tbsp butter
1 large onion, chopped
2 jalapeno peppers, chopped
2 tbsp vegetable oil, or as needed

4 (10 inch) flour tortillas
1 C. shredded Mexican cheese blend

Directions

1. In a large skillet, melt the butter on medium-low heat and sauté the onion for about 10 minutes.
2. Add jalapeño peppers to onion and cook for about 10 minutes.
3. Transfer the onion mixture into a plate.
4. In the same skillet, heat about 1 tbsp of the olive oil in the same skillet and place 1 tortilla.
5. Top the tortilla with 1/4 C. of the Mexican cheese blend, 1/2 of the onion mixture and 1/4 C. of the Mexican cheese blend.
6. Top with 1 tortilla and cook for about 1-2 minutes per side.
7. Repeat with the remaining oil, tortillas, cheese and onion mixture.

FRENCH QUARTERS
Quesadillas

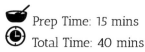 Prep Time: 15 mins

Total Time: 40 mins

Servings per Recipe: 4

Calories	598 kcal
Fat	35.9 g
Carbohydrates	47.7g
Protein	22 g
Cholesterol	64 mg
Sodium	967 mg

Ingredients

1 tbsp canola oil
2 andouille sausage links, finely diced
1 poblano chile, finely diced
1/2 red bell pepper, finely diced
1/2 large red onion, finely diced
1/2 C. frozen corn kernels
4 flour tortillas

2 C. shredded Colby cheese
1 tbsp canola oil
1/4 C. sour cream (optional)
1/4 C. salsa (optional)

Directions

1. In a large skillet, heat 1 tbsp of the canola oil on medium heat and cook the diced sausage, poblano pepper, red pepper, red onion and corn for about 15 minutes.
2. Place 1/4 of the sausage mixture on one half of each tortilla and top with 1/2 C. of the cheese.
3. Fold the tortillas to make a half moon shape.
4. Repeat with the remaining ingredients.
5. In a large skillet, heat 1 tbsp of the canola oil on medium heat and cook the quesadillas for about 5 minutes per side.
6. Cut each quesadilla into 4 wedges
7. Serve with a topping of the sour cream and salsa.

October's
Quesadillas

Prep Time: 10 mins
Total Time: 1 hr 10 mins

Servings per Recipe: 6
Calories	470 kcal
Fat	18.2 g
Carbohydrates	59.2g
Protein	17.5 g
Cholesterol	40 mg
Sodium	1003 mg

Ingredients

2 sweet potatoes, scrubbed
6 (10 inch) tomato flavored tortillas
2 C. shredded sharp Cheddar cheese, divided

1 (15 oz.) can black beans, rinsed and drained, divided
1 C. salsa (optional)

Directions

1. Set your oven to 450 degrees F before doing anything else.
2. Cut several slashes into each sweet potato.
3. Cook in the oven for about 45 minutes.
4. Transfer the hot sweet potatoes in a heatproof bowl and immediately, mash them.
5. Now, set the oven to 200 degrees F.
6. Heat a skillet over medium heat and warm a tortilla for about 2 minutes.
7. Flip the tortilla and sprinkle with about 1/3 C. of the shredded Cheddar cheese about 1/2-inch from the edge.
8. Let the cheese melt and spread about 1/3 C. of the mashed sweet potato, followed by 2-3 tbsp of the black beans.
9. Fold the tortilla in half, enclosing the filling.
10. Repeat with the remaining tortillas.
11. Keep the filled quesadillas warm in the oven.
12. Serve in the wedges topped with salsa.

POTLUCK
Quesadillas

Prep Time: 20 mins
Total Time: 35 mins

Servings per Recipe: 4

Calories	987 kcal
Fat	58.7 g
Carbohydrates	77g
Protein	32.9 g
Cholesterol	105 mg
Sodium	1692 mg

Ingredients

1 lb. lean ground beef
1/2 onion, cut into 1-inch pieces
1 C. barbeque sauce
4 flour tortillas

1 C. shredded Cheddar cheese
1 C. French-fried onions

Directions

1. Set your oven to 350 degrees F before doing anything else.
2. Heat a large skillet on medium-high heat and cook the beef and onion for about 5-7 minutes.
3. Drain the extra grease.
4. Stir in the barbecue sauce and cook for about 5 minutes.
5. Spread 1/2 of the ground beef mixture over a tortilla and top with 1/2 of the Cheddar cheese and 1/2 the French-fried onions.
6. Top with a second tortilla.
7. Repeat with the remaining ingredients.
8. Place the quesadillas onto a baking sheet.
9. Cook in the oven for about 5-10 minutes.
10. Cut into triangles with a pizza cutter.

Breakfast
Quesadillas

🍳 Prep Time: 10 mins

🕐 Total Time: 25 mins

Servings per Recipe: 2	
Calories	380 kcal
Fat	5.7 g
Carbohydrates	78.5g
Protein	6.2 g
Cholesterol	0 mg
Sodium	473 mg

Ingredients

1 Honeycrisp apple, diced
2 tbsp light corn syrup
1 tbsp honey
1 tbsp maple syrup

1 pinch ground cinnamon
1 pinch brown sugar
2 11-inch flour tortillas

Directions

1. Heat a large skillet on medium-low heat and cook the apple, corn syrup, honey, maple syrup, ground cinnamon and brown sugar for about 8-10 minutes, stirring every few minutes.

2. Transfer the apple mixture into a bowl.

3. In the same skillet, place 1 tortilla on medium-low heat and top with the apple mixture evenly.

4. Top with the remaining tortilla and cook for about 1-3 minutes per side.

ALMOND
Hope

Prep Time: 15 mins

Total Time: 15 mins

Servings per Recipe: 36
Calories	241 kcal
Fat	15.7 g
Carbohydrates	21.9 g
Protein	5.6 g
Cholesterol	5 mg
Sodium	77 mg

Ingredients

2 lbs white confectioners' coating
1 C. peanut butter
2 C. dry-roasted peanuts (or almonds)
3 C. crisp rice cereal

2 C. miniature marshmallows, optional

Directions

1. Melt your confectioner's in a microwave. Then add in the peanut butter and work the mix. Add in the cereal and marshmallows then layer dollops of the mix onto a cookie sheet covered with wax paper.
2. Put everything in the fridge until it is all cold.
3. Enjoy.

Made in the USA
San Bernardino, CA
20 December 2019